WRITING THAT CHANGED U.S. HISTORY

U.S. CONSTITUTION

by Josephine Larsen

pogo

Pogo Books, an imprint of Jump! Library by FlutterBee

Ideas for Parents and Teachers

Pogo Books let children practice reading informational text while introducing them to nonfiction features such as headings, labels, sidebars, maps, and diagrams, as well as a table of contents, glossary, and index.

Carefully leveled text with a strong photo match offers early fluent readers the support they need to succeed.

Before Reading

- "Walk" through the book and point out the various nonfiction features. Ask the student what purpose each feature serves.
- Look at the glossary together. Read and discuss the words.

During Reading

- Have the child read the book independently.
- Invite them to list questions that arise from reading.

After Reading

- Discuss the child's questions. Talk about how they might find answers to those questions.
- Prompt the child to think more. Ask: Why does the United States need the Constitution? Is there anything in it you would change? What and why?

Pogo Books are published by Jump!
3500 American Blvd W, Suite 150
Bloomington, MN 55431
www.jumplibrary.com

Jump! is a division of FlutterBee Education Group.

Library of Congress Cataloging-in-Publication Data is available at www.loc.gov or upon request from the publisher.

ISBN: 979-8-89662-352-6 (hardcover)
ISBN: 979-8-89662-353-3 (paperback)
ISBN: 979-8-89662-354-0 (ebook)

Editor: Alyssa Sorenson
Designer: Emma Almgren-Bersie

Photo Credits: National Archives, cover (document), 5, 16; mato181/Shutterstock, cover (flag); Olga Galushko/Adobe Stock, 1; BillionPhotos/Adobe Stock, 3; Everett Collection/Shutterstock, 4; Howard Chandler Christy/Architect of the Capitol, 6–7; ungvar/Shutterstock, 8; VectorMine/Adobe Stock, 9; Science History Images/Alamy, 10–11; SAUL LOEB/AFP/Getty, 12–13 (top); Fred Schilling, Collection of the Supreme Court of the United States, 12–13 (bottom); Sundry Photography/Adobe Stock, 14–15; SeventyFour/Shutterstock, 18; North Wind Picture Archives/Alamy, 19; Alan/Adobe Stock, 20–21; Viktoriia/Adobe Stock, 23.

Printed in the United States of America at Corporate Graphics in North Mankato, Minnesota.

TABLE OF CONTENTS

CHAPTER 1

A NEW GOVERNMENT

The United States became a country in 1776. It fought for freedom from Great Britain in the Revolutionary War (1775–1783). It needed a strong new government.

U.S. soldiers

British soldiers

Articles of Confederation

Leaders wrote the Articles of Confederation in 1777. This document said **Congress** would make laws. But it did not say states needed to work together. No one made sure laws were followed.

Leaders agreed to change the document. George Washington was one. He and others met in May 1787. They started writing a new document. It is the U.S. Constitution. It has rules. It explains how the U.S. government works.

DID YOU KNOW?

Fifty-five men wrote the Constitution. James Madison, Alexander Hamilton, and Benjamin Franklin were some. It took them four months.

George Washington
U.S. Constitution

CHAPTER 2

"WE THE PEOPLE"

The Constitution starts with the words, "We the People." It means the United States is a **democracy**. People work together. They make decisions as a group. Why? The leaders did not want one ruler to have all the power.

The Constitution has seven parts. They are called articles. They explain the three branches of the U.S. government. The Constitution says they must share power.

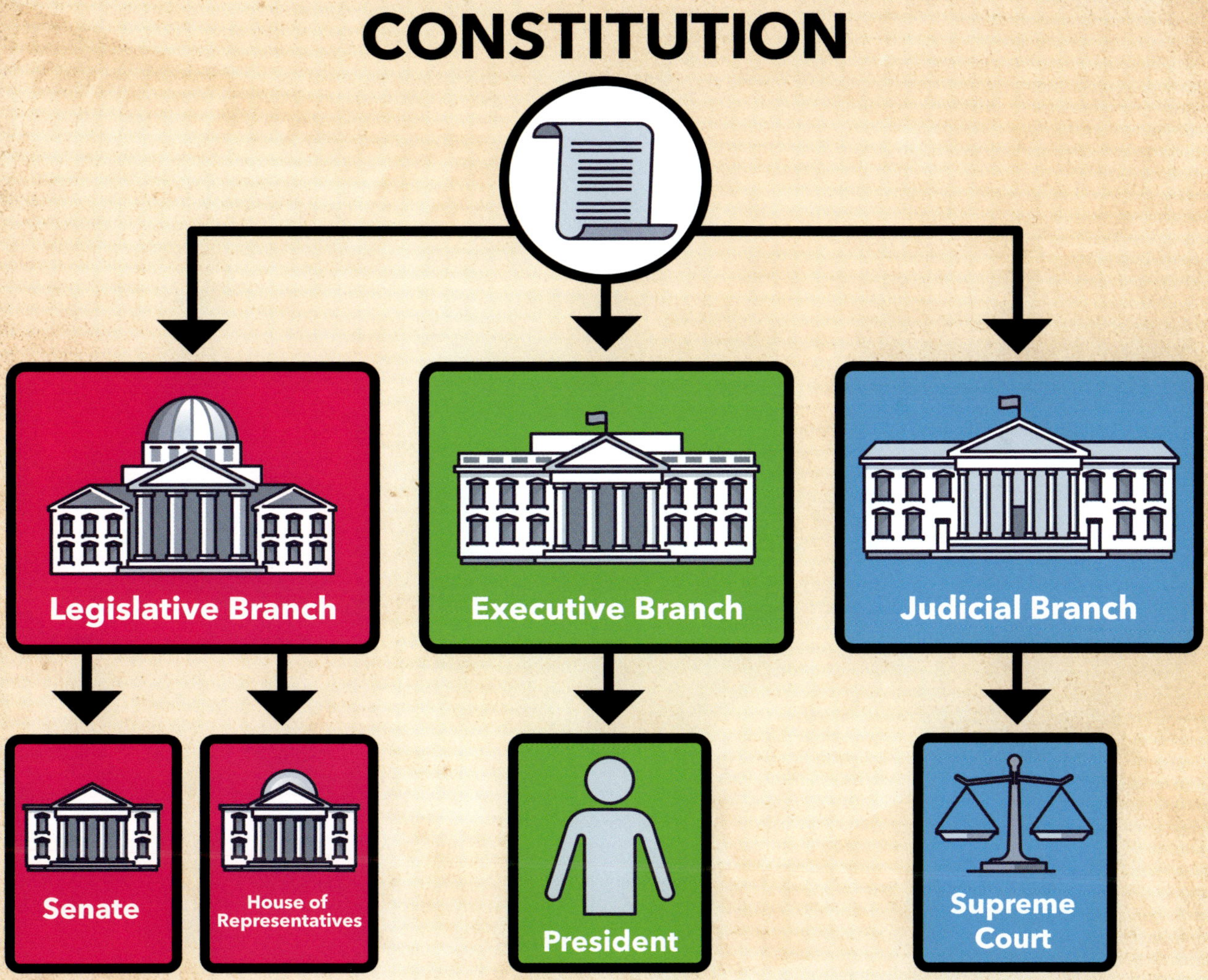

CONSTITUTION

Legislative Branch

Executive Branch

Judicial Branch

Senate

House of Representatives

President

Supreme Court

IN GOD WE TRUST
Congress

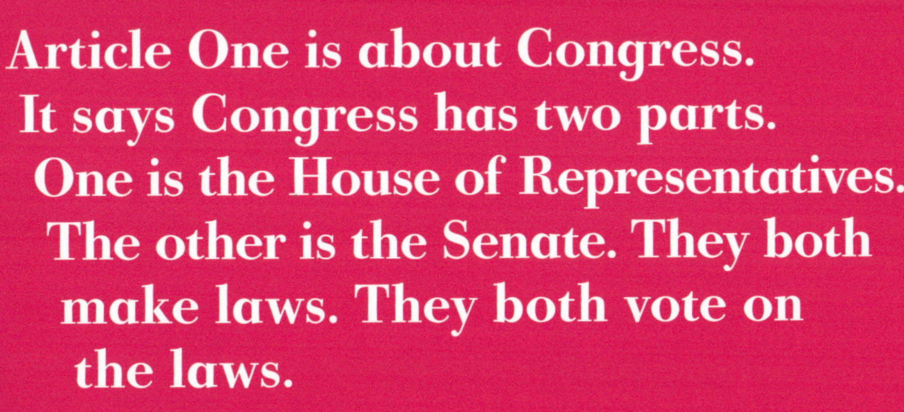

Article One is about Congress. It says Congress has two parts. One is the House of Representatives. The other is the Senate. They both make laws. They both vote on the laws.

WHAT DO YOU THINK?

Each state has two Senators. States with more people have more members in the House of Representatives. Do you think this is fair? Why or why not?

Article Two is about the president and vice president. It says how **candidates** are **elected**. Americans vote for them.

Article Three is about the **U.S. Supreme Court**. **Justices** decide if laws follow the Constitution.

WHAT DO YOU THINK?

The Constitution has three rules about who can be president:

1. A president must be at least 35 years old.
2. They must have been born in the United States, or their parents must be U.S. **citizens**.
3. They must live in the United States.

Do you think there should be more rules? Why or why not?

2024 candidates for president
Supreme Court justices

SHERIFF

Article Four says states can make their own laws. But they must work together in some cases. Like what? They must help each other catch criminals.

Article Five has rules about **amendments** to the Constitution. The House, Senate, and states must all vote on the changes.

Article Six says the Constitution is the country's highest law. All other laws must fit within its rules.

Article Seven explains how the Constitution was **approved**. When it was written, there were 13 states. Nine of them had to agree to it.

signatures

TAKE A LOOK!

What were the 13 states when the Constitution was written? When did each state approve it? Take a look!

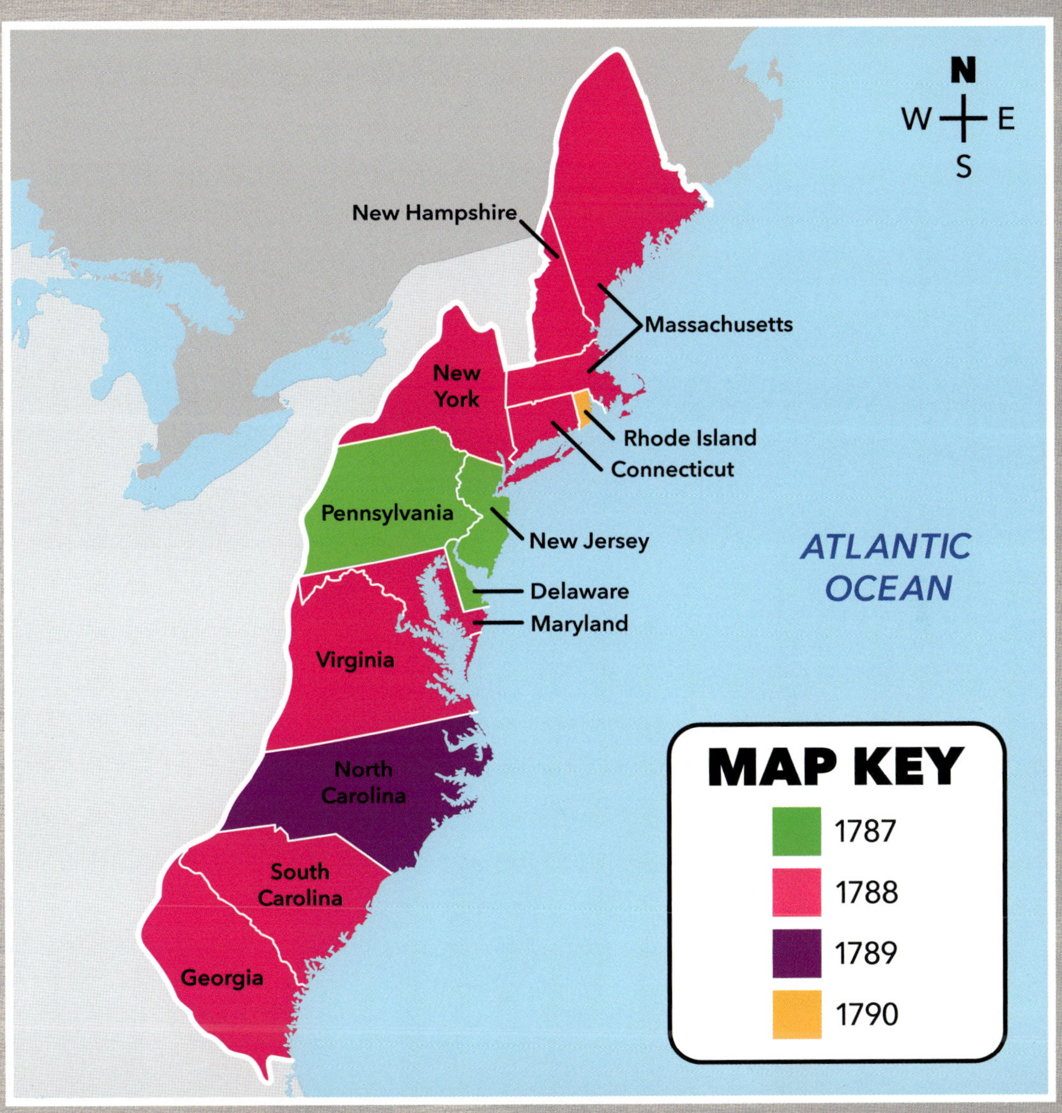

CHAPTER 3

MAKING CHANGES

The Constitution can change. The first 10 amendments were made official in 1791. They are called the Bill of **Rights**. They gave Americans rights. Freedom of speech is one.

As of 2025, the Constitution had 27 amendments. They show how the United States has changed. In 1865, the Thirteenth Amendment was added. It said **slavery** was not allowed. People celebrated.

Some amendments give people more rights. In 1919, the Nineteenth Amendment gave women the right to vote.

The Constitution is the country's most important document. It created a government that still works more than 200 years later. What would you add to the Constitution?

QUICK FACTS & TOOLS

TIMELINE

What are important dates in the history of the U.S. Constitution? Take a look!

1775–1783
The United States fights for freedom from Great Britain during the Revolutionary War.

1776
The United States becomes a country.

NOVEMBER 15, 1777
Congress passes the Articles of Confederation.

MAY 25–SEPTEMBER 17, 1787
Leaders meet to talk about writing the U.S. Constitution. The meeting is called the Constitutional Convention.

SEPTEMBER 17, 1787
Leaders sign the U.S. Constitution.

JUNE 21, 1788
New Hampshire is the ninth state to approve the U.S. Constitution. This makes it official.

DECEMBER 15, 1791
The Bill of Rights is approved.

GLOSSARY

amendments: Changes made to a law or legal document.

approved: Officially accepted.

candidates: People who want to be chosen for a job or role, like president.

citizens: People who belong to a country and have full rights.

Congress: The part of the U.S. government that makes laws.

democracy: A type of government in which people choose their leaders by voting in elections.

elected: Chosen by people who vote.

justices: Judges on the Supreme Court.

rights: Things you are allowed to do.

slavery: The practice of forcing people to work in harsh conditions with no pay.

U.S. Supreme Court: The highest U.S. court that upholds the U.S. Constitution and laws.

INDEX

TO LEARN MORE

Finding more information is as easy as 1, 2, 3.

1. Go to www.factsurfer.com
2. Enter "U.S. Constitution" into the search box.
3. Choose your book to see a list of websites.